Get off the Stage and on to Business

The concise book on how a top spokesperson can push your profit over the top

Elsje van Jaarsveld

Copyright © 2014 Elsje van Jaarsveld

All rights reserved.

ISBN: -10:1495907414
ISBN-13:978-1495907418

AUTHOR'S MESSAGE

In my life of broadcasting and managing a corporate communication department, I have seen both sides of the media – the media itself and the desire of a corporate company to be recognised in the media. I have learned what companies are doing wrong in their dealing with the media and how easily they can correct those mistakes.

I noticed the huge value that a brilliant communication department can have on a company's profit but that some corporate management styles are tripping the value that a communication department can add.

With this book I aim to inform business owners, corporate managers, and boards of directors how to tap into this incredible resource called communication but also how to manage it in such a manner that the communication department can literally add a few numbers to their profit.

As business people are very busy in general, I wrote this book in a concise and to-the-point manner to give all the necessary information in a short period of time.

Feel free to visit the website to take advantage of the bonus articles:
www.GetOfftheStageAndOnToBusiness.com

Contact the author:
Tel: +27 (0) 82 5380 212
Email: elsjevj@gmail.com

CONTENTS

	My message	i
1	Two Worlds collide	Pg 1
2	The Boardroom: The talk	Pg 4
3	The Boardroom: The talk outside the boardroom	Pg 9
4	The Boardroom: The talk inside the boardroom	Pg 14
5	The Boardroom: The boardroom's own newsroom	Pg 19
6	The Newsroom: The journalist's job description	Pg 24
7	The Newsroom: Going to the media	Pg 27
8	The Newsroom: Sugar coat the begging	Pg 32
9	The Newsroom: Light's, camera, action	Pg 37
10	The Newsroom: From boardroom to newsroom	Pg 42
11	The Strategy: Putting everything together	Pg 45
12	The Strategy: When the media turns sour	Pg 49
13	The Strategy: The next step	Pg 51
14	Bonus article: Let's get practical	Pg 53

ACKNOWLEDGMENTS

Printed and distributed by

Createspace, an Amazon Company

1 TWO WORLDS COLLIDE

Any businessperson would know that the environment plays an enormous role on any business' success. A farmer might depend on the rain for a big harvest, the number of pupils of a school can be influenced by job opportunities for their parents in the area, or a hair salon might take a knock if women don't have money to spoil themselves anymore. A business simply doesn't operate in isolation. Each group of an organisation that might have an influence on the business or are influenced by the actions of a business are called **STAKEHOLDERS**.

If a business doesn't enjoy the stakeholders' buy in, a business will not perform as intended. Imagine a company which tries to improve its customer service but is busy with retrenchments… the skeleton staff will surely not be motivated to walk even further for a client if they already have to work over time to make up for too little personnel.

Without getting too technical, I just want to quickly name the different stakeholder groups and subjects a company will most likely have: clients, shareholders, authorities, suppliers, employees, general public, activists, and labour unions. For each company, the influence of the stakeholder will be different. For example, a mining company will not only have to think about their shareholders' pocket, but also about how their actions might influence the nearby communities. Will there be more air pollution? Can the communities benefit from job creation at the mines? and so forth.

Communication towards these stakeholder groups is extremely important to the sustainability of the company, as stakeholders can sabotage a strategy if the stakeholders aren't motivated to support it. Communication is the only tool to explain the reasoning behind the intended strategy and to motivate the stakeholders to act in an ideal manner.

Therefore, a thorough communication plan should be developed -- as part of strategic planning -- to communicate with these stakeholders, which will include what to say and how to say it. The board will determine what must be said, but a top spokesperson must implement the "how" portion.

In case the "how" is not executed by a top spokesperson, the stakeholders might get angry, and the intended strategy will definitely not be realised. There are many ways to communicate with the stakeholders, but a lot of aspects influence the success thereof. You might have the ideal plan to communicate with the public using a media platform, but will the media run your story or ask the right questions on air? It can easily turn against you.

This book will shed light on why communication to particular stakeholders is important and how it can be done to show results. This book will explain what the responsibility of the board is and what most certainly is not. It is quite important that you appoint a top spokesperson, not simply an adequate one, to push your profits over the top.

To give you a sneak peek on how a communication plan looks, I have included a framework for a communication plan on my website. You might just use it as a template for your business. Have a look at it at www.getoffthestageandontobusiness.com.

2 THE BOARDROOM

THE TALK

The talk with your employees is crucial, and if you are in business for some time, you know all the reasons why employees are so important. Now, your communication to your employees impacts their morale in a big way. The board's communication to the employee may be achieved in different ways. It can be done by a monthly meeting, company newsletter, or introduction videos, but a direct manager may also be the sole channel of communication. Unfortunately, companies may overlook this crucial factor. I worked at quite a big company that built an employee newsletter into their strategy. It was a very noble thought, but it was given to an employee that had several other tasks. So, she couldn't make it her main focus. I experienced it first-hand that businessmen underestimate the amount of work that goes into a publication, even if it is a four-page publication, and then they can't understand why it is of low standard. A publication must be the focus of an employee's job description in order for the publication to be well-written and beneficial for the company.

The result of this publication that was dealt with on the side, so to say, was a publication full of spelling errors and with a terrible layout. The interest in this employee newsletter was very low for obvious reasons, and the board of directors didn't want to waste their precious time to try and correct it. I was very disappointed at the time, as I had only graduated a few months back, and all the theories of why an employee newsletter was necessary were fresh in my head.

So why is an employee newsletter necessary? It builds company culture, it informs the employees of corporate strategy, it creates buy-in for certain projects, it lifts the spirit after an economic shock, it prepares employees for a tough time ahead, and it creates unity. Can I ask you something at this point, business men and woman? Is it possible for your company to go without these things? If an employee newsletter can mean that your employees will give their cooperation for a very important project, why do companies treat the publication as a side dish?

A few years later, I got promoted at the company, and I had the chance to turn the publication around. We had to employ a writer and a fantastic graphic designer, from a person who had to compile the newsletter by herself together with all the other work, to a whole team that worked on it. In the end, this newsletter was always on time, visually attractive, and written in plain but neat language. It was fun to read, and the personnel looked forward to receiving *their* newsletter.

However, there was one thing that still bothered me at the time that I left the company. The newsletter was still not what I wanted it to be. If the purpose of the newsletter was to inform employees about corporate strategy and future projects, the board of directors needed to be part of the editors of the publication to give their input on what must be reported on. I just want to be clear that directors must not just sign the newsletter off after the communication team has put their best effort into the publication. The directors must treat the publication as if it may go out to shareholders or clients.

The most dangerous thing about a sub-standard personnel newsletter is that personnel will stop reading it. If a newsletter is your primary communication tool with your personnel, you are in serious trouble, because how will you communicate to them regarding that extremely important project that can maybe make or break your company?

I suggest having a primary communication tool such as a personnel newsletter or a video channel, or whatever works for you, but that you also create a fun channel. My communication team and I did a small test on the communication channels that we managed, and we found that people react to, and therefore read, fun articles or projects. So, what we did was to make all the articles fun; whether it may be accompanied by a very attractive picture or a very colourful layout, make sure it is fun.

A personnel newsletter may not always make way for the fun stuff, so create another channel, such as small notice boards, everywhere in the office. Make sure you change the posters constantly to keep employees interested and portray different messages in a fun way. This will definitely get them talking and engaging in office projects. This is what builds unity and keeps their spirits high.

Every company's needs differs, but the crux is that you create a channel through which you can communicate effectively. I say "effectively" with a reason. Stories need to be compiled differently for different mediums. For instance, if you want to convey a story by video, the text will be in conversational form; if the medium is a poster, the message will be accompanied by an illustrative picture with little wording.

Communication tools do not only require common sense to implement;; this is actually a science, and much research has been done on this topic. So, please don't give this powerful task to your secretary. Contract it to a professional communication practitioner.

The professional communication practitioner or spokesperson will also manage the communication towards the personnel in such a manner that they don't get overloaded. Communication overload is an easy trap to fall into. Personnel receive emails, newsletter, attend meetings, see posters, etc. If these channels don't convey the same message (in a different format) at the same time, personnel will get confused and won't be able to take the desired action. A professional communicator will manage all of these messages so that the business can profit from the personnel's behaviour.

When a previous employer of mine had just started their communication department, they expected fireworks. Therefore, we developed firework-strategies, but the structure of the company didn't support the communication strategy well enough, and the result was politics, politics, politics, and more politics. The company recruited a very competent man to start the department but really didn't give him the right competent personnel, supportive structure, and adequate technology. It was similar to a very competent man without any hands. But the company still expected fireworks. They didn't have the insight at the time that you have gained so far by reading this book.

The communication to the personnel formed an integral part of our firework-strategy, and we embarked on a monthly personnel newsletter, interesting notice boards, and personal visits to our clients. But imagine this nifty strategy on a screw structure infused by politics and drama. It is simply a recipe for disaster.

My plea here is that you, as a business owner, will give the same attention to a communication department as you give to the financial department, because I am very sure that your numbers will not be outstanding before your relationship with your stakeholders is outstanding.

3 THE BOARDROOM

THE TALK OUTSIDE THE BOARDROOM

Clients are the stakeholders that bring in the monthly income, am I right? And you want them, not only to visit you, but to *re-visit* you. The re-visit has much to do with your relationship with your client because if they already visited, you at least met each other. From there, a relationship starts, am I right?

I first want to distinguish between marketing and communication. Although these two things work closely together, each has different goals, in my opinion. Marketing has to get the client in your store or get a client to use your service or product, but communication is to keep the client engaged. Communication equals a relationship. Marketing tends to be one-way. You can't talk to a billboard or to a television ad. Communication is two-way. You can comment on a company's Facebook page. That is engagement.

Another way to explain is to distinguish what is paid for and what is worked for (with a little payment). A pamphlet is paid for – it is marketing, a radio advertisement is paid for – it is marketing, but a consumer magazine is worked for (besides the printing cost that you spent) – it is communication.

Communication is a marketing tool, and marketing is a communication tool, because you can use communication to market your product, and you can use marketing to enter into communication with your client. For example, a consumer magazine, which is communication, runs an article on a story that serves as marketing. A billboard advertisement mentions the Facebook page and therefore the company wins "likes" on the Facebook page and can engage with those Facebook fans.

Communication and marketing definitely work back and forth, but marketing is another science and beyond the scope of this book. It is very important to attract the right people, and that is the most important responsibility of marketing.

Communication, on the other hand, is to build a relationship with the people that are attracted through marketing initiatives. Sometimes the marketing action is eliminated; it really depends on the situation. Especially non-profit organisations can only make use of communication – but I know you are in a hard main stream business, so we focus on that.

By now you will agree that your communication department isn't the marketing department as well; the two only work together closely.

To get your clients to revisit your business, the relationship needs to be nurtured, and this we do by effective communication. We need to engage our clients in our business operations and let them feel their voice counts and that they really enjoy our highest priority. If you manage to engage the client, it will serve as a major competitive advantage over your competitor because you won't lose the clients. Some will go -- it is the nature of business -- but you will keep the majority of your market.

It will most certainly happen that a business will slip up here and there, but if you have a relationship with the client, the client will have the confidence to tell you when you make a mistake and grant you the opportunity to correct the mistake.

I remember, a few years back, a major car manufacturer had to pull a specific product, and one of my colleagues was affected by this disruption. The manufacturer came to fetch his car and replace it with another product. When asking my colleague if he had lost any confidence in the brand and if he would get himself another vehicle elsewhere, my colleague's response was quite astonishing to me. He said he would stay with the brand, even more than before, because the company had the decency to protect his life against any manufacturing failures that might cost the manufacturer millions. What I didn't know is that representatives of the company spoke to him often, before the incident, to make sure he was still happy. So the company had a strong relationship with the client (my colleague) and therefore they could survive the incident.

The same principles of building a personal relationship with a friend applies to building a relationship with your client. Some people like to constantly speak to their clients, some only like a cup of coffee every now and then, and for some, a deep conversations once a year is enough. In the spectrum of your clients, different clients with different personalities will be present. You will not know what their likes and dislikes are. What your responsibility is is to cater for the media usage. Do they use print media? Which print media? Magazines or newspaper? Which newspaper and how frequently? Is there a portion of your clients that only use online media? Social media or research on websites? Or do they respond to a personal email?

The identification of your clients' media behaviour is extremely important because if you don't crack the code, so to speak, you will definitely be off on the wrong foot. It will be a massive loss of an enormous amount of labour and money, so make sure to get this right. How will you get this right? Well, it is a science, and the top spokesperson knows the science. Leave it up to the person that you appointed, but see that you appoint the top spokesperson that you need.

Your communication practitioner will know where to find the research on your clients' media usage. I can imagine that the appointment of the top spokesperson might be a headache for you, so please make contact with me via my website so that I can help you to stay on the right track.

Sometimes a communication practitioner isn't allowed the space that is needed to be the top spokesperson. In my view, this happens when the spokesperson doesn't serve as a senior manager. I mean, if a spokesperson has a cardinal key to your profits, why push that person down? Anyway, this happened to me. Our clients wanted print media. They engaged through personal conversations with us, so we managed a consumer magazine and meetings with the clients, but the CEO wanted an electronic newsletter. It was trendy, I believe. Our department just needed to make it work. On top of all the important work, we had the weight on our shoulders to make another publication see the light. If you have never worked in a newsroom, you will not begin to understand the amount of work that goes into the preparation of the systems of a publication, the building of the audience, and then gathering content for the publication. It was a bi-weekly publication as well, so it was a major burden. Don't do that to your communication practitioner. Why would you do that if you went through all that trouble finding the top spokesperson?

The other side of the coin is also true. The communication initiatives that the spokesperson embarks on must produce results. There are a few ways to measure the success of communication campaigns, and my suggestion is that you keep your spokesperson accountable to the goals that were mutually agreed upon. The social landscape is also constantly changing, so what seemed to be a success the previous year might not produce the same results this year, thus must any spokesperson include an evaluation plan in the proposed strategy, and you must stand true to it.

To give you an idea of possible measuring methods to communication projects is to look at the size of the audience of a channel as well as the frequency of engagement of the audience. Just keep in mind that the measurement can't always be presented in numbers, but it will definitely give you an indication of the success of the project.

4 THE BOARDROOM

THE TALK INSIDE THE BOARDROOM

At some stage in your life you will have something to present to an audience whether it might be a room full of clients, employees, or colleagues. I want to dedicate this chapter to how communications can help you in the boardroom and how your top spokesperson can support you to really get the buy-in from your board.

I assume that the message you want to get across to management is a sound business idea or a new project or maybe a solution to a particular problem. You may determine the message, but your spokesperson needs to package it; this is what the spokesperson's job is, mostly in any given situation.

First of all, we need to evaluate the amount of information that the board possesses regarding the situation. Were the board present during the occurrence of the problem for which you want to propose a solution? Why does the board want to hear about your business idea? Do they need cash flow? Were you given the task to develop a new project strategy?

When you determine what the board's motivation is regarding your presentation, you need to start at that point. Otherwise your whole presentation may start off on the wrong foot, the reason behind your presentation will fly out of the window, and nobody will be motivated to listen carefully. This is why you also might have experienced a lack of interest in your projects in the past.

Sometimes the board didn't even instruct you to give a presentation, and you request it yourself. In these instances, you first need to state to the board why they need to listen to you. Make sure that the reason for your presentation is reason enough for them to listen to you, otherwise you could have rather spent your time on the golf course.

There are different ways to state the reason for the presentation, but it can be straight forward. Don't disguise it in extravagance; it must be short and to the point to grab your audience's attention in a flash.

We believe that you have your audience's attention at this point, and now the journey starts. A journey is literally what this is. A journey, because you need to take your audience to the place you want them to go. First you need to get them walking, and that is when you paint the background of the situation.

This phase calls for the research that you have done regarding the issue that you will talk about. The way you present the research must be interesting, because no matter how motivated the audience is to listen to you, it is only human to get side-tracked when somebody just reads a lot of research.

Here your top spokesperson can be a huge help. In my opinion, you can just give him or her the research and let them make it work. Show pictures, videos, use demonstrations, or even get an employee to quickly talk about his or her experience with the problem the presentation aims to address. The thing is, more often than not, you will be speaking to people that are not specialised in your area of expertise. You are the expert, and you must give your audience the background of the problem or project, just like your varsity lectures explained the study work to you. But the preparation of such interesting explanation takes an awful lot of time which you don't have. Well, you don't have to do the preparation; grant the opportunity to your top spokesperson.

Then the journey will continue where you have to keep your audience present but also give them a glimpse of the end. You see, they can easily lose interest at any given time, and to give them a glimpse of the end will keep them motivated to listen to you. You can do this by reminding them what the outcome can be, what goals you are working toward, and how your presentation relates to the reason of the presentation.

Only now your audience will be ready for your presentation. Now you can dig into your strategy and get the board talking. Remember to constantly link an action plan to the outcome of the strategy. Remind the board what goals are being addressed by doing a specific action. The presentation doesn't really have to contain a conclusion. This is not a speech; it is the presentation of a strategy. What you want to achieve is the board to get talking about your strategy and for certain decisions to be made. Therefore, your presentation will result in a conversation in the boardroom, and once they have made up their mind, they will continue with the agenda. The only conclusion of the strategy is most likely the implementation thereof. This is a brilliant tool to get the buy-in from your colleagues, and when you have the buy-in, a project is on the way to success. Without the buy-in of the board of directors, I would rather book myself a holiday. (Actually not a bad trade.)

A few years back, a senior manager, at a previous employer of mine, wanted to change the packaging of the products in his division and I had to help him with his presentation to management. Once approved it would be a huge project and require a lot of capital. The senior manager had a background in branding and communication, so he understood the value this project could add to the product. However, his audience didn't have the branding and communication background that he had. They were financial and legal gurus and couldn't see why they should throw hundreds of thousands of rand towards the project if they already had packaging. I must say that the packaging at that time was horrible. Nothing looked the same, and the consumers couldn't link the product to our brand. To improve the profit, the branding should have changed, but the board couldn't see into it.

In the end, the senior manager pulled through, and the board granted their approval even though it had been very difficult to persuade them. What did we do to persuade them? We took them on a journey. First of all, we took pictures of the product in the stores comparing it to the product right next to it. This served as the background coupled with a lot of textbook research. What worked best were case studies presenting the figures of how other companies succeeded with their new product packaging. Then we had to produce life-size samples of the new product packaging and compare it to the current packaging. It was really a big mission to compile that presentation, something that you might not have time for. But you need the result of a great presentation, and, therefore, you need a top spokesperson. Don't compromise on this; I believe you agree that you will sell yourself short if you try to spare the spokespersons' salary.

5 THE BOARDROOM

THE BOARDROOM'S OWN NEWSROOM

This chapter is probably the most important chapter of the book, or let me rephrase: the implementation of the principles in this chapter can result in extraordinary communication to your client and media coverage. So, pay attention.

The concept is to build your own newsroom within your company. This newsroom will be managed similarly to a media-house, publication, or programme – it depends on your strategy. The sole responsibility of your company's newsroom is to build channels to reach your stakeholders and to constantly push the stories through these channels. This is quite challenging.

The development of each channel is similar to the development of a TV channel or newspaper because it has to get the in-house operations in place, get the stories up to standard, and build an audience. To build an audience, people need to want to read or listen to your stories, but since your newsroom is only pushing company news, the building of an audience might be very difficult because not all employees want to read or listen to those particular stories.

So, what is the recipe? The appointment of a top spokesperson. The spokesperson will have the knowledge to portray the stories in an interesting way and add attracting stories to the company news in order to lure the employees, clients, or shareholders to the particular channel. Even more, the age of the stakeholders will differ and therefore will their use of media differ. Youngsters may be very engaged in social media while shareholders might demand the content on a hard copy. Shareholders may feel that media is more creditworthy when it is in print.

Now, the spokesperson will need to push the same story through different channels, but each channel calls for a custom-made story. Imagine a long story, meant for print, is pushed through Twitter (which only allows 140 characters per tweet). To make media landscape worse is that the media landscape is changing constantly. Ten years ago we couldn't imagine a virtual social area. Therefore, the spokesperson must stay ahead of times. It is a full-time job!

Some managers think that a newsroom can be managed by one person, but is a newspaper a one-man show? If you want the newsroom to produce state of the art communication channels, then the communication department need the tools to deliver.

First of all, the people employed in the newsroom must be trained in order to perform in the newsroom. A newspaper has an editor, sub-editors, journalists, graphic designers, and advertising consultants -- you can skip on the latter if your company newsletter doesn't accommodate advertisements. So, if you try to establish a company newsletter, then you need an editor, sub-editor, journalist and graphic designer in the newsroom.

A production house, one that produces broadcasting programmes, employs a producer, production manager, production assistant, writer, camera and sound personnel, and an editor. If your strategy is to communicate to your stakeholder via an in-house TV channel, then you need these functions. If you don't have these functions, my honest suggestion is that you contract the company newsletter to a professional media agency.

In my early career, our so called newsroom had to compile a monthly newsletter. The newsroom was decentralised and each person was operating independently. The personnel not only had to do the company news, but also the branding and marketing of the rather big company, which was already too much to handle. So the result was that the company news was only "part" of our jobs; it didn't enjoy centre stage. The implication of a company being a side job is a sub-standard publication and loss of audience.

A few years later, the company wanted a brilliant showcase consumer magazine to be published bi-monthly focusing on stories that our clients would find interesting, and then act so that we could generate more revenue. It worked extremely well, but to make that jump from a struggling publication to a showcase magazine, we certainly had some changes to make. The first thing was to move the company news to a high priority in the department. We couldn't employ extra people at the time, so we had to sub-contract the publication to a professional media agency which had all the resources. It was still very important to manage the content closely, so I acted as the editor of the publication, and we invited key people in the company to our editors meeting. This way we could manage the content, but the media agency made it work. Their writers, graphic designers, sub-editors, and advertising consultants worked on our publication.

Making use of an agency can also tilt the other way if an inadequate agency is appointed for the job. We had to compile an orientation DVD for new employees. Anyone would know that this is a costly exercise, but nevertheless, we gave it a try. A few quotes for producing the DVD came in from different agencies, and off course, we took the cheapest one; it wasn't only the cheapest one but was way cheaper than the other quotes. Although we hadn't worked with them in the past, the price was so good that we immediately accepted. It was the worst thing I ever did in my entire career. I had to evaluate each little image and ask for changes to be made. For the time I spent on the changes, I could have learned the software myself and done the whole project even quicker comparing to how long it took in the end. In hindsight, it would have been better to choose another channel to communicate to the new employees, a channel that could be developed cheaper than a DVD but still be done thoroughly.

It is very important to remember that each media agency has its own speciality, and when appointing a media agency, you should research the agency's speciality. Your strategy should be compiled by the board of directors in conjunction with your communication manager, who is hopefully a top spokesperson. The communication manager will then delegate the tasks to either the in-house newsroom or to a media agency whose speciality the specific task is -- for instance, give the task of a company magazine to a media agency that has done it for thirty years. I digress, but you hopefully get my point.

GET OFF THE STAGE AND ON TO BUSINESS

Now I want to touch on social media. Social media has became a communication channel just as important as broadcasting or print media. It has its own character that for sure poses an opportunity. It is extremely fast, so in a crisis situation, it is the perfect channel to speak to the relevant stakeholders, given the channel has the right audience. But -- the big but -- there must be someone who is solely responsible for your social media. Because people talk to you via social media, they can also bad mouth you via social media, and this can escalate within minutes if not picked up and attended to. How would I know if I need a social media strategy? It really depends on your stakeholders and their media behaviour. If they use social media, so should you.

I haven't explained the big deal as to why you need a newsroom. It is a simple answer: a newsroom generates coverage in the mainstream media. You see, the top spokesperson will link the in-house channels to the different media groups, and they will pick up on a story automatically. More on this in the chapter entitled "Putting Everything Together".

6 THE NEWSROOM

JOURNALIST'S JOB DESCRIPTION

It is common knowledge that a journalist covers stories, but there are different types of journalists. The way that a television journalist completes his or her work is sometimes worlds apart from that of the newspaper journalist. Journalists normally work within a beat, whether it may be on lifestyle, agriculture, or politics; it differs. Even if two journalists work for the same publication but on different genres or beats, their work is different.

Let me give you a broad overview to explain. A newspaper may be only local, so it covers local news, therefore it will carry news that touches the lives of the local community. A national newspaper that focuses on politics and business will report on that: politics and business. Therefore, the journalists for the national newspaper would be political journalists and business journalists. That is the format or style of that newspaper. Another example: lifestyle television programme will interview beauty icons and interior decorators. The television presenter may not even have a journalism degree, but may rather be a former model.

Now the picture may become more clear to you that every publication or programme has a topic and that the journalists have a very specific instruction to fill the space, whether it be airtime or space in the newspaper, with stories true to the topic of the publication or programme.

I worked at a weekend breakfast show that reported on business, politics, food recipes, and celebrities. That is all the show covered. However, we received hundreds of requests to cover charity since we had an enormous viewership. We couldn't cover these charity stories because we needed to stay true to our format.

You see, a programme or publication builds its audience by staying on track with the format or topic because that is the reason people keep watching or reading. The people like the topic, and they expect that particular topic when they return. The moment we fall short of the format, the audience will be disappointed and we will lose them. It is not that we were horrible people not wanting to cover the charity stories; it simply didn't fit into the style of the show.

A publication or programme is managed like a business because it is a business. The publication or programme is a product, so every producer will evaluate what stories will be covered, and the infrastructure of the publication or programme will be designed accordingly.

At the breakfast show, we had a business reporter and a news editor to report on stories; that is all. Our budget was designed around this concept, so how would it have possible to report on charity stories if we hadn't even employed a general journalist? Luckily, not all the programmes and publications are the same. Some may cover only charity stories.

We can even go a step further. Sometimes one country has a few business newspapers, but they carry different stories; how is that possible? What is news for the one publication may not be news for the other publication because of their audience. One publication may carry news for property developers, and the other one may report on shares. Certainly there will be stories that may be seen in both publications but in a different way. One may report on the worldwide economic crisis and how it will impact property development, and the other one may also report on the worldwide economic crisis but will report on how it may impact shares.

Now that you have a broad picture of how publications sort their news stories, the next chapter will show you how to interact with the different forms of the media to get your story out there.

7 THE NEWSROOM

GOING TO THE MEDIA

The previous chapter introduced you to the different media platforms and how the world of journalism works. This chapter will explain how you can use that information to your benefit. Once you read it, it will probably seem like common sense, but if nobody tells you, how would you know?

Previously I spoke about how journalists choose their stories. They have a very specific topic or genre that they work with. This topic is determined by the style or format of the publication or programme that the journalists work for. The journalist who works for a political publication must cover political stories. What do you think will happen when you send a story about a school nursery project to this journalist? You will only be disappointed. But what would happen if you send this same story to the local newspaper? They will eat it up.

In order to get your story in the media, you must choose the media platform carefully, otherwise, you will end up making media calls and getting no interviews or stories in the press. Choosing a platform is the first and foremost factor to consider when approaching the media, but there are several other factors to consider.

We can distinguish between hard and soft news, and aging news and classical news. Hard news is murder, business, politics, mostly current affairs. Soft news is on the lighter side of life; it might be a story on a new school that opened or a new cure for cancer. Aging news is just what it says. It is news in the now; next week it will be old and aging, like a ship that has sunk. Next week everybody knows it, and there is no more meaning to run the story. Classical news is information that will always stay relevant, for instance, how a specific training program can better performance.

Certain publications and programmes mostly cover hard news, and since this news ages quickly, the publication or programme will be published on a high frequency. Journalists in these fields work in a high speed environment. When will a company be in need of such a publication or programme? When a crisis occurs. The crisis might be a fire in a certain store or an employee that got hurt on site.

Crisis situations can create chaos in a minute, and if the public isn't notified of the correct information almost immediately, this can ruin your reputation. It is recommended that a professional spokesperson handles these situations, as one word can lead an interview in a direction that you wouldn't prefer. A spokesperson will establish a crisis centre, but this is a topic on its own. I would like to elaborate on this topic, however, so I have included information on this in the chapter entitled "When the Media TurnsSour".

I would like to explain the beauty of classic news. The media is normally fed with a lot of stories relevant to the publication or programme, but, believe me, there are times that there seems to be happening nothing in the whole world. That is the golden moment for you to slip right into the media coverage. Every journalist that does a good job has a database of relevant stories. Whenever a "quiet news day" occurs, the journalist will dig into that database to fill in the gaps. Journalists are almost daily on a deadline, and there is absolutely no excuse of not having something to fill the space with. So this database is a lifesaver. Therefore, you must make sure that you are in the database and that the story that you deliver is timeless.

The journalist will also choose the story that needs minimal editing. You must remember, this journalist is probably on a very tight deadline. My suggestion is that you write a press release on your story in such a way that the journalist can almost publish it as it is.

Once again, you will need a professional to write the article on behalf of you. You will only be giving the person the facts. What is the use if you give the facts to a journalist but the article doesn't get published because there was no time for the journalist to edit your version? The fee that you pay the professional spokesperson is very small in comparison with the huge pay-off you my get from getting published.

The more the journalist fiddles with your article, the bigger the chance of a mistake. This happened to me once in national media where I sent a press release in Afrikaans (a language spoken in South Africa). The journalist had to translate it to English, perhaps under great pressure. Nevertheless, the translation wasn't exactly accurate, and the statement of our CEO in a national publication was somewhat false. This is a simple mistake that could cause major embarrassment. Don't let it happen to you. Give this task to a professional spokesperson, and don't underestimate the amount of work that releasing press releases are. Be prepared to pay for this service. It will surely serve you well.

Another important factor to keep in mind when approaching the media is to make sure your story stands out from the rest. It must report on something different, from day-to-day stories or at least a new concept. Journalists receive hundreds of stories, but I must say, they go through the stories to find that one article that fits them well.

Sometimes you must be prepared to pay to make the story happen to get coverage in turn. A previous company that I worked for had a training program that they managed on their own costs. The testimonials of people that followed this program were absolutely astonishing, and it was a very unique concept. There wasn't a day when we had to market this project at our own cost. The media was calling almost weekly to schedule interviews. We were on TV, in magazines, and newspapers, and we did absolutely nothing. We just handled the media requests.

The above is a perfect example of a story that interested the media, that fit well into different publications and programmes, and was very, very unique. It was almost like a roller coaster. When the media first heard about us, the other programmes and publications followed spontaneously.

At this point, I must say that handling media requests is another skill set, because the media wants you to act immediately. If you are a manager that can't act quickly, the media will lose interest, and the momentum of media requests will soon die.

8 THE NEWSROOM

SUGAR COAT THE BEGGING

You seriously must sugar coat the begging in order to run your story. You want to splash your story all over the country and most likely spend money to make the story a reality. Unfortunately, you are very dependent on journalists to run the story, but you can do a few things to improve your chances to getting media coverage.

First, it is important that the right channel is identified for your specific story. I already mentioned this, but to recap: a lifestyle story most probably will not get coverage within a hard news publication or programme. If it is a lifestyle story, send it to lifestyle programmes or publications. This is the most basic step. Otherwise, you will most certainly be disappointed and waste your time.

You know by now that different channels exist: television, radio, magazines, newspaper, and social media. There are other channels like expos and conferences, but these will not give you that instant media coverage, in my opinion. Therefore, I will only advise you to concentrate on television, radio, magazines, and newspaper. I presume that you have your own social media channel through which you can run the story anyway, so I will leave that out as well.

Once you have decided which channels you will be using to distribute the story, you will have to inform the different platforms of the story. This you can do by releasing a press release; drop it on your social media page or hold a press conference, but the latter is sometimes difficult if key people can't attend. You can send the press release to key persons and drop the story on the social page with a link to the press release. This is probably the quickest and most effective way to make the story public in a short period of time.

If the channels that you identified are interested in the story, they will use it in different forms. Television is a slower medium, especially if we talk about a weekly show and not the news that goes out every hour. But let's presume that you have a story that concerns the environment, and you send it to a weekly environment show. If the story can be of use in a month's time, they may not make contact immediately but will visit you in three weeks to make time to prepare the insert very well.

Radio is a very, very fast medium; the story may go onto the air the same day that you send it, but it must be of interest for them. The radio host can ask you to come in for a live interview, live telephone interview, or prerecord your interview and broadcast it in an hour's time. So, if you send your press release to radio, be prepared for very quick reaction.

Newspapers are also a fast medium, but they are bound by the amount of pages that is determined by the amount of advertisements. If a big story breaks, it will enjoy priority, and the newspaper may not have place for your story due to too little advertisements. If your story is still valuable tomorrow, it may be published. So make sure the story is still of good news in a week's time, as it is now to ensure your place in a newspaper whenever they have place, However, it may also happen that your story never gets published if the story is totally classic and can be of value in six months' time as well. Then, other more urgent stories may always be a higher priority.

Magazines are quite a slow medium,; it depends on the frequency of it being published, but to give you an idea: I was editor of a magazine that was published bi-monthly. We had an editor's meeting four months prior to every issue, and then we discussed stories that we had already identified prior to the meeting. Thus, a story might only see the light in four or five months from identification. Not all magazines are bi-monthly magazines, but they are still a slower medium than newspapers and radio. However, magazines are the medium to run a story if you would like to explain a story in very much detail.

If you need to get a story out immediately, my suggestion would be to inform the radio stations' newsrooms first. A radio's infrastructure enables journalists to run a story in a matter of hours, but it will be a short information clip. If you need a detailed explanation of a story, I would go to a weekly newspaper or a magazine.

I would like to give you a little bit of an inside scoop on how news travels between journalists in order to help you to understand the path your media release will walk. Once you have submitted your press release to a channel, the channel will decide whether they like the story or not. If you are lucky, it will be published in a short bulletin. From there, the newsroom may decide to investigate the story a bit further, and they may call for interviews to make a bigger story of it.

Once a specific programme or publication has used your story, another channel may pick up on it and change the angle of the story to run a follow-up story. The model of a story is that different channels may use the story in different formats at different times. At a previous employer of mine, the communication department sent a very short story to a weekly newspaper. The national radio station picked up on it and called for further interviews. This is a spot on example on how two channels used the same information in different formats. It served us well.

I do, however, have examples of media releases that didn't produce results at all. A previous employer of mine spent a lot of money on an environmental research study. We thought the media would scoop it up, but the opposite was true. Everything on our side was spotless -- the media release, the arrangements for a media conference, everything. In the end, our story was published in only one medium, and it didn't enjoy the amount of space in the magazine as we assumed it would. Luckily, we had our own magazine that had a terrific readership, so we could publish the story on our own. You will never know how the media will use your story, but if you go through the trouble to build your own media channel, you will always have the assurance that your story will be heard by the stakeholders that need to hear it.

Remember, you absolutely have no control of the story once it is in the open, so make sure you are ready for inquiries. The media may also call different parties to get their view of the story, so it may not always be in your favour. For example, you inform the media of a social project that you launched to improve the lifestyle of pupils in your area. The media may call the school head, and his opinion may be that the project excludes the poorer pupils and that he doesn't give his support to the project. This may cause a great deal of criticism, and it can spiral totally out of control. Therefore, my suggestion again is to appoint a top spokesperson that will have sound judgement on how the public and media may react.

The idea of a press release might scare you off, but it is really just a basic article of what the story is all about. You must include the answers to these different questions:

- What question: *What happened?* Or *What project is planned?*
- Who question: *Who did it?* Or *Whom will embark on the project?*
- When question: *When did it happen?* Or *When will the project take place?*
- Why question: *Why did it happen?* Or *Why will the project be started?*
- Where question: *Where did it happen? Where will the project take place?*
- How question: *How did it happen?* Or *How will the project be managed?*

The shorter and more concise the press release, the easier for the journalist to use it. Don't think that fancy words will persuade a journalist to use a story. The journalist will make his or her decision based on the nature of the story. Just make sure all the facts in the press release are correct and that the contact information is included to enable the journalists to investigate the story further. To give you examples of a standard press release, I included a few of my press releases on my website. You can download these examples for free.

9 THE NEWSROOM

LIGHTS, CAMERA, ACTION

You are probably asking: so how do I get myself or my company representative on television or radio? The answer is very simple: you have to create something that interests the media, and then you must tell them about it. The not so simple answer is: what interests the media in order for me to create it? This is really the key to getting your company in the media.

People normally believe one needs to know a journalist or news editor to get coverage, but what do you do if you don't know any journalists? It is really easy; just contact the advertising department of the specific publication or programme and ask to be transferred to a journalist. The advertising department will always take your call, and it will even be better if you already have a relationship with an advertising agent from doing business with them in the past. Sometimes advertising must be regarded as buying good will to get coverage in a later stage, but, and this is another big but, even if you have bought good will in the past, if you still don't have a story that the journalist is interested in, you will not get coverage.

You informed the media of a story, and the media reacted, granting you an interview. So this is the big interview, or so you presume -- the live television interview, or it may even be pre-recorded. One thing I want to emphasize is that you must treat any interview as if it was a live interview, because once it is recorded, you have no power over it to make sure your words are edited. Editors and journalists are normally under a tight deadline, and time allows minimal editing. A competent journalist is normally the one that gets it right the first time. So, don't comfort yourself in presuming that the interview is pre-recorded and can be edited afterwards.

A journalist will cover a story from a certain angle. The angle may be about whom a story is, like the death of Nelson Mandela. The whom is the most important. A story can also by covered from the what angle. What happened? A brilliant example is the 9-11 happenings. The first sentence for such a story would be exactly what happened. Other stories can have a why angle, a when angle, or the how angle. The story's first sentences or the journalist's first words will indicate the specific angles of the story.

Keeping this in mind, you can sort of predict the direction of an interview if you know what angle the journalist will take on the story. Journalists will be more than willing to discuss the angle of the story beforehand with you. Make sure that your preparation is also guided by the angle of the story, but remember: a journalist has a certain amount of airtime available for the story, and he or she will be instructed to fill that time. This means that if the angle of the story is covered, the journalist can go into other questions as well. For example, if the angle of a story is the whom angle, and you answered all the questions about the whom, the other questions will follow. These questions will be: what happened? when did it happen? why did it happen? how did it happen? Thus, be prepared for the other questions as well.

Television and radio interviews are the easiest interviews to prepare for since stories for broadcasting are a lot more concise than for press. Magazines and newspapers allow for detailed coverage. To illustrate this, I inserted a real radio news bulletin below. Take note that this is the whole story for radio purposes.

The coach of the national soccer team announced his final team that will represent the country during the world cup. The announcement came after the date of the world cup was made public this morning. Several parties commented on the new coach's choice, labelling it as the most surprising choice in the history of soccer.

The above is the whole radio bulletin regarding this story, but believe me, it will be covered in detail in a newspaper. This radio bulletin consists of forty-seven words, but you can expect a story of approximately three hundred to five hundred words in the newspaper.

This is why I am saying that an interview for television or radio is actually nothing to worry about if you are well prepared

Journalists can catch you off guard, and there are ways to work around that as well. The most important thing is to stay calm, otherwise you can't even get the words out that are so simple to say. My honest suggestion would be to get somebody to do this on behalf of you if cameras and microphones aren't exactly your thing. You see, literally hundreds of thousands of people may see or hear that interview that offers an enormous marketing opportunity for your company, but it can also tilt the other way and shatter your reputation into millions of pieces.

One mostly forgets that the public couldn't care less who talks to them regarding your company as long as the person can give all the information they want, and if it is done in a warm, relaxed manner, you can win over a lot of new customers. People normally think that they must be perfect on the screen or on radio, speak perfect English, or use impressive words. Nothing is further from the truth. The moment you aren't yourself, the audience will pick up on it and lose interest. It is such a relief to have the permission to be yourself on screen, but you must still be alert and respectful towards your audience.

Another benefit of a radio interview is that you can have your notes in front of you, but don't make the mistake to write your whole speech and try to deliver it word for word. The listeners will immediately feel the distance, and you will be much more stressed. Just write keywords that you can pick up on, and if you forget something, just continue; it is not the end of the world.

Just one last tip for radio interviews: if the scene of a studio and microphones are nerve-racking for you, ask the journalist to phone you instead. It can easily be done, and you will be able to sit in the comfort of your office, having your notes ready and doing the interview. It will feel like a normal telephone conversation with your best friend.

One day I had to support one of the company's managers while doing a pre-recorded interview. Prior to the interview we arranged that I would have certain questions ready to remind him what he wanted to say, and I was also prepared to drop some keywords which he could pick up on. I tried everything to put him at ease, but he was extremely anxious. He made the biggest mistake: he prepared his speech word by word, and he got more stressed when he lost his words or swopped a word. I never got a chance to ask any questions, and the interview looked staged and very impersonal. Don't do this! I cannot say this enough. For this manager, it would have been much better to ask somebody else to do the interview. I believe the guy prepared the speech in too much detail since his notes was his only safe haven. Unfortunately, there are no safe havens in the broadcasting media, so if you need a safe haven, rather get somebody else to step into the media.

I hope that this chapter set you at ease for that big television interview. If this only scared you more, you know what to do. Get that top spokesperson!

10 THE NEWSROOM

FROM BOARDROOM TO NEWSROOM

You picked this book up probably hoping to gain some insight on how to get your word in the media. Although this book shows some strategies to communicate with the media, I strongly suggest to get a professional spokesperson to do certain tasks. I can imagine that this might be a new concept for you, because how can somebody else speak on behalf of you to the audiences that your business serves?

The thing is your audience will probably not know that it is not you who are speaking. Your communication will be channelled through different platforms, so who would know who is at the back of the platform? For instance, if you decide to create a consumer magazine, a column can be created where you speak to the clients. Your photo will be there, and your name will be at the bottom of the article, but do you need to write the column yourself. Or can you share your ideas with a professional communication practitioner who compiles the article for you? It will still be your voice because it is your ideas, but do you think it is absolutely necessary to use you precious time to do something you are not really good at? I think you agree that a professional can take care of this.

What about radio and television appearances? If somebody does the interview on behalf of you, the public wouldn't expect the managing director in particular to do the interview. The person who handles it can be introduced as the spokesperson of your company, and as long as the spokesperson has all the information to answer the questions, the public will be more than happy to listen.

The beauty of a spokesperson is that this person knows exactly how to prepare for a radio or television interview, so the spokesperson will facilitate the whole preparation. She or he will ask you the certain questions, and you can provide the answers that you already know. The spokesperson will use your answers as the content for the interview.

Whenever a journalist continues with a story to fill the time, the spokesperson may use different techniques to handle it professionally. Answers such as "that matter is still being investigated" or "the board is busy discussing it" or "we know the public is eager to know more about it so we will publish the answer on our website within the next two days" are brilliant ways to answer a question vaguely but still answer it enough for the interview. This is also a brilliant technique to use in order to get follow up interviews. The spokesperson will go back to you, get all the information that is needed for a follow-up, and then schedule a follow-up interview. What more can you ask for?

In case you contract a spokesperson and not hire full-time, it is important to stick with one person as long as you can. The public will get to know the person as your business' spokesperson, and it will appear as if the person is employed full-time. It is also advisable to keep the spokesperson in the loop of decisions and happenings around the business. When the spokesperson is employed full-time, you might consider allowing that person into your board meetings. Sometimes a decision is made on a director's level that may not have a desired effect on the public's opinion, and the spokesperson will immediately make you aware of it.

At a previous company that I worked for, the board decided what the increase in salaries would be the next year. The worker unions were very unhappy with the rate and took it to the media which bad-mouthed our company nationally. I heard about the happening a day or two before the media covered the story, so there was no time to prepare for the chaos. We were in a very tight spot because now we could only react towards allegations. We looked like the bad guys. If I had had the chance to prepare for the media crisis, I could have notified the media myself of the reasons for the company's decision, and they would have handled the story much differently. If I had been allowed in the boardroom, I could have spared the company's reputation.

11 THE STRATEGY

PUTTING EVERTHING TOGETHER

Now you know that a spokesperson can do your writing and speaking, but it all starts with a strategy, a communication strategy that is aligned with your overall corporate strategy. That brings me to another point. If the spokesperson is to consult you on a communication strategy but the corporate strategy isn't revealed or finished or fall shorts in any way, how is the spokesperson supposed to make a success of the communication strategy? Thus, include the spokesperson in boardroom-level decisions.

You must also consider that a communication strategy takes more than one year to show success since communication channels need to be built, and it takes a while to build an audience for a specific channel. It would therefore be the best to incorporate a communication strategy into the long-term strategy of the company.

Let us say your spokesperson created a top of the art communication strategy. You will probably be wondering how it will be executable if the person is not employed full-time. There will most certainly be contact with your company on a regular basis, and my suggestion is that it will be you or another director that oversees this function and an administration employee to handle day-to-day activities.

The communication strategy will probably consist of a few publications. It might be a personnel newsletter and a consumer magazine. There can be introduction videos included and a strategy for press releases and more.

The beauty of a publication or programme is once the format is set, the content must just be entered into the set format. Once you have signed off the format, the content must be entered regularly. Your involvement will stretch as far as an editor's meeting where you will decide what content must be included. The administration person will supply the facts, and the spokesperson will make the publication or programme work.

There is a continuous process that needs to be repeated hundreds of time to build an audience and make a success of the communication platform. My point here is: you will be a decision-maker. That is it, and you can require feedback from the spokesperson to evaluate if strategy is still intact. There are a few techniques to measure the success of a communication platform, but I will not go into detail here as it will be the responsibility of the spokesperson.

To keep these communication channels up and running is a major task. Lots of small information will come in daily, and it needs to be directed accordingly. Sometimes the facts of an article need to be verified, and the spokesperson will have to probably take a chunk of her or his day to achieve that. At the end of a day only one sentence might be verified. The reason I am saying this is to emphasize the amount of work that goes into the communication strategy. If these small tasks aren't performed, the publication will be sub-standard, and your audience will lose interest. That is why I advise that you hire or contract a spokesperson to take care of this side of business. There is more to it than just words; it is a science. That is why a spokesperson is qualified to do the job correctly.

Another huge benefit of having a few communication channels that work like an oiled machine is that media coverage will almost happen spontaneously. A good spokesperson will have the savvy to automatically link your communication channels to handpicked journalists.

You may have an electronic newsletter that can also be sent to a journalist who might have interest in the stories that are covered in the newsletter. The journalist can be added to the distribution list, and whenever your spokesperson publishes the newsletter to your clients, the journalist will also pick it up, automatically. The spokesperson may not even remember about the journalist being on the distribution list and may receive a call from a journalist, out of the blue.

In the chapter entitled "A Journalist's Job Description", I wrote about a training program of my previous employer that got so much media attention. This is exactly how it started. We had a small story in the company newsletter about the training program, and the media picked it up because they were linked to the newsletter. From there, the journalists picked it up in other publications, and the television heard about it, and the rest is history. The story snow-balled, and we only had to handle the request from the media.

Unfortunately, there will be company news or information that you desperately want to get out, but the media is simply not interested. It is news for you, but for them it is not. What must you do in such a situation? I hope that your spokesperson will have designed a channel to speak to your clients; it may be a consumer magazine, YouTube channel, or even a social media channel, as long as it has the audience that you want to speak to. If this is the case, you can publish the news in this channel and then you don't even need the formal media. Use your own media. If you don't have an existing channel for the specific audience, I suggest that you pay for the publicity. It can be in the form of an advertisement or a promotional article.

A company that used this technique brilliantly is a company that defended a massive media crisis. Rumours were spread through social media, and the company was desperate to silence the chaos. The next day, a full page advertisement was published in many newspapers. The company used the advertising space to write an article. The letters were big so that the reader would get the message, short and concise with only the logo of the company at the bottom. I thought this was a brilliant way to get publicity in a flash.

Although the company probably had to pay for the advertisement, they saved their reputation in a flash, and business could continue as usual.

12 THE STRATEGY WHEN THE MEDIA TURNS SOUR

A business doesn't always seek media attention, especially if something bad has happened and it is better to keep quiet. Unfortunately, the media has the ability to find out about the bad happening and want to inform the broader public about the matter. This can turn into a nightmare and literally destroy your reputation that you built for the past twenty years. Fortunately, this media publicity can work in your favour if handled correctly, but a top spokesperson is absolutely unnegotiable for this purpose.

As a business owner you will know what the media will be after in your industry. It might be wage negotiations, safety of personnel, money matters, and so forth. Whatever it is, you need to have a plan in place for when the media pitches. The strategy must emphasize who is authorised to speak to the media in this case; it needs to point out what the role of the communication department must be in such a case. It will also have to discuss where press releases will be distributed and if a media conference will be necessary.

Once a strategy is developed, it must be implemented before the crisis happens, meaning the personnel must be informed on what they must do if they receive media inquiries. Keep in mind that the media will not be nice when you are in the wrong. They can pitch at your store or ask the most junior employee for a statement. Therefore, all personnel must be informed what needs to happen in such a case. But how do you educate a thousand employees on the matter? Well, luckily you have a very popular employee newsletter by now where you can publish articles to teach the employees.

The development of a communication strategy is a very technical subject, and your top spokesperson will need to develop it for your company. The spokesperson also has to implement the plan and take charge once a crisis strikes the company. Thus, before you land in hot water, appoint the spokesperson so that you can be ready for any communication crisis.

By now, I believe you would agree that a top spokesperson can take your business to new heights. I hope you take this advice and get that top spokesperson on board, right away. If you don't know where to start finding that top spokesperson, I will be happy to help you. Simply visit my website or see the "Author's Message" at the beginning of this book for my contact details.

13 THE STRATEGY

THE NEXT STEP

This book has elaborated on several topics, and you may be confused what to do next. First, evaluate who your stakeholders are. Next, evaluate where you are at the moment in terms of your communication to the different stakeholders.

If there is no communication to the stakeholders, then you should develop a communication plan from scratch. Visit www.GetOfftheStageAndOnToBusiness.com to download a copy of my framework of a communication plan.

To develop a communication plan is definitely a science, and my suggestion again is to appoint a top spokesperson to help you with the process. If you are in the dark on whom to appoint, I would help you with this process. Feel free to make contact with me via the official book website.

Maybe you already have a communication plan, and it is being implemented. In this case, you must closely evaluate if the strategy is producing the desired results, since it can be a costly exercise in terms of money and labour. It needs to deliver! There are several ways of evaluating the success of communication activities, but each communication plan is very unique, and to explain the different evaluation techniques will form a book on its own. The best way to deal with this is to ask the help of a professional spokesperson with the evaluating, even if you already employ a communication practitioner. The evaluation is a major task and your communication practitioner is most probably too busy to look after this very important aspect. Therefore, get a top spokesperson to evaluate your current communication status and do a presentation on what can be improved. Thereafter, you and the board can decide what instructions to give to the communication practitioner.

If the budget is tight at the moment, I would suggest that you hire a top spokesperson only to present a strategy and evaluation plan, and be prepared to pay for that service, but that you then appoint a junior communication practitioner to implement the strategy. The top spokesperson can evaluate the process on a three months' basis.

If you still are in total darkness regarding the communication activities, visit the website to contact me with regards to strategies, implementation, and evaluation of the communication resource.

14 BONUS ARTICLE

LET'S GET PRACTICAL

I include this last chapter just to give you a few pointers on writing and delivering a speech, but my suggestion is that if you feel that you don't have the talent to do it yourself, that you rather ask somebody professional. I hope by this time you are persuaded that communication can be an extremely valuable tool building in your business and that it is absolutely worth the money to hire a professional.

When writing and delivering a speech, your only goal is to give the audience information that they need in such a manner that it is valuable to them. Writing a speech is all about the message, so first of all, you must ask yourself who the audience will be. Is it personnel, shareholders, clients, general public, the media, or other groups? Once you have confirmed who the audience is, you must ask yourself what the audience needs to hear. This is where the message comes in. Is it a motivational speech, simply informational, or do you need to persuade them to a certain opinion? This will be your starting point.

Then you must establish at what level you must speak to them, meaning how much does the audience already know about the subject. You don't want to irritate the audience with basic information if they already are aware of that. In fact, they will feel that you underestimate their intelligence.

Keep in mind that your audience will only attend your presentation if they need the information that you promise to give during your speech.

The next step is to gather all the information on the topic which you feel to discuss with your audience. You need to include background information, real stories, anecdotes, and research for a well-rounded presentation. Then choose only three main ideas of the topic. Remember: a speech is an introductory to something to stimulate interest. If the audience feels they want more information, they will investigate the matter themselves. You mustn't feel that you need to include everything in your presentation; you only need to give the highlights and elaborate on main ideas. If your presentation is too long, the audience will forget what you have said, and you will not reach your main goal.

Order the information within the framework of the three main ideas. Which research, stories, and anecdotes go with what ideas? Keep it logical and simple; don't try to be too fancy.

Then, write an introduction and conclusion. Your introduction needs to tell the audience what your presentation is all about and what main ideas will be discussed. The conclusion will remind the audience what you spoke about and what the main ideas were. Try to include a bit of humour in the introduction and conclusion; this will instantly lift the audience's morale and motivate them to listen to your speech. There are a numerous other methods to develop an introduction or conclusion, but my experience is that humour is the most effective. If you are really not funny, don't try to do it artificially. Rather start with a quote or anecdote.

How to deliver the speech is also part of the writing process because you will have to determine what support material you will use when delivering the message. When considering the different support material, keep in mind what you are most comfortable with. There is no rule that a Powerpoint or a white board makes you the best speaker. What makes you a great speaker is the way the audience experiences you, and you must be very natural in front of that audience. You must speak with the audience and not to the audience. You must have a conversation with the audience and not simply deliver a monologue. So, use your own words, be who you are when you are at the office, be yourself.

I had the task to teach personnel about delivering speeches in front of clients because conferences were part of our marketing strategy. Now, these employees were very specialised in technical stuff but never had to communicate to an audience. I could teach them the basic stuff: speak loudly, look at the audience, don't speak too long, arrange your speech in a logical manner. Some employees were better than others, but it was okay because it wasn't a public speaking competition. It was merely a technical presentation. On the other hand, there were personnel that couldn't do it at all, and it wasn't that they were incapable of doing their work; it was just a case where a spokesperson rather had to make another plan. A short video could do the trick or an article could be handed out, but management kept those employees in front of the audiences.

In my opinion, these conferences could have been much more effective if a spokesperson had the authority to manage the conference by his or her sound judgement.

DEAR READER

I hope by reading this book you have gained a lot of insight on how a top spokesperson can push your profit over the top. I also believe that now the communication subject is more clear to you regarding its scope of influence on your business, the amount of work and time it requires, and the intensity of the planning that goes into communication strategy development.

Futhermore, I really hope that this book has given you a few pointers on how to deal with your communication department, and that they will enjoy as much attention as the financial department enjoys.

Be blessed, be successful,

Elsje van Jaarsveld

ELSJE VAN JAARSVELD

ABOUT THE AUTHOR

With the very rare combination of having corporate experience and working in broadcasting, Elsje is the perfect person to tell you how to get your company's message across effectively. She has an intense passion for business and communication, and these have always been the drive behind her endeavours. During Elsje's career, she headed a corporate communication department, acted as editor of industry-related magazines, hosted a TV show, and is doing radio work.

At a very young age, Elsje's natural talent for public speaking got herself winning places at national competitions. She was also chosen to represent South Africa, as a spokesmodel, at the World Championships of Performing Arts in Los Angeles, America.

Elsje holds a communication management degree, and further studies are business related.

With her unrivalled talent coupled with her studies and experiences, Elsje is truly a top spokesperson.

www.ingramcontent.com/pod-product-compliance
Lightning Source LLC
Chambersburg PA
CBHW071808170526
45167CB00003B/1216